Did Yo

GLOUCESTER

C000022015

A MISCELLANY

Compiled by Julia Skinner

With particular reference to the work of Chris Witts

THE FRANCIS FRITH COLLECTION

www.francisfrith.com

Based on a book first published in the United Kingdom in 2004 by The Francis Frith Collection®

This edition published exclusively for Bradwell Books in 2013
For trade enquiries see: www.bradwellbooks.com or tel: 0800 834 920
ISBN 978-1-84589-548-8

British Library Cataloguing in Publication Data

Did You Know? Gloucester - A Miscellany
Compiled by Julia Skinner
With particular reference to the work of Chris Witts

The Francis Frith Collection
6 Oakley Business Park,
Wylye Road, Dinton,
Wiltshire SP3 5EU
Tel: +44 (0) 1722 716 376
Email: info@francisfrith.co.uk
www.francisfrith.com

Printed and bound in Malaysia
Contains material sourced from responsibly managed forests

Front Cover: **GLOUCESTER, FIRST SUNDAY SCHOOL 1892** 29907p

The colour-tinting is for illustrative purposes only, and is not intended to be historically accurate

CONTENTS

GLOUCESTER, SOUTHGATE STREET
1900 45508

INTRODUCTION

The splendid tower of Gloucester's cathedral rises above the roofs of Gloucestershire's county town, forming an important part of the city's skyline. A monastery was founded at Gloucester in Anglo-Saxon times, but it was the 11th-century Serlo, Abbot of Gloucester, who founded the present cathedral seen today; he energetically raised funds for buildings which were to be not only grand but also sumptuous, and the magnificent structure has been augmented and restored over the succeeding centuries.

Gloucester has been an important crossing point on the River Severn since ancient times: the site was the first point on the river where a bridge could easily built. In the Roman period it was an important city, and became the commercial centre of the Severn valley.

The layout of medieval Gloucester can still be seen in the city centre, where the four main roads, Westgate, Eastgate, Northgate and Southgate Street meet and form the main focus of the city centre, watched over by St Michael's tower. Before the tower was built, an old stone cross stood here (it was removed in 1754), and the area is still known as The Cross; the roads lead away from here to the old city gates of Gloucester.

Queen Elizabeth I gave Gloucester the formal status of a port in 1580, but it was not until the completed construction of the Gloucester and Berkeley Canal in 1827 that the city began to equal Bristol in importance as a grain port with three commodious docks, the largest of which was opened in 1892. Trade through the docks declined in the second half of the 20th century, but the docks area has now been preserved and restored, and is a major heritage attraction for tourists. The history and heritage of the city can also be followed on a special walking route around Gloucester that has been developed, called the Via Sacra (meaning 'Sacred Way'), which follows the old city walls and is denoted with dark paving slabs.

GLOUCESTER, THE CATHEDRAL, SOUTH PORCH
1892 29901

GLOUCESTERSHIRE DIALECT WORDS AND PHRASES

'Adry' – thirsty.

'Airsens' – haws, the berries of the hawthorn tree.

'Artishrew' – the harvest mouse.

'Asker' – a newt.

'Badger' – a dealer in commodities in olden times, ie a butter dealer was known as a 'butter badger'.

'Candlemas bells' – snowdrops. (Candlemas Day is February 2nd.)

'Chubby' – the hedge-sparrow.

'Dabbly' – wet, rainy.

'Emmet' – an ant.

'Flummock' – a slovenly, untidy person.

'Ladycow' – ladybird.

'Maggot' – a magpie.

'Mugglement' – a state of muddle and confusion.

'Nettlesome' – quarrelsome.

'Watty-handed' – left-handed.

GLOUCESTER, THE PARK, THE FOUNTAINS
1912 65115

7

GLOUCESTER, THE DOCKS 1950 G20052

HAUNTED GLOUCESTER

Gloucester has been listed as one of the top ten most haunted cities in Britain. Here are just a few of its haunted places:

The New Inn in Northgate hit the news in 2010, when a full pint glass mysteriously levitated from a bar table (where no one was sitting) and fell onto the floor. The event was witnessed by many customers who were taking part in a pub quiz, and was also caught on the pub's CCTV. This was just one in a number of strange events which have occurred at the pub in recent years, prompting the Gloucester Active Paranormal Society to investigate. The pub building dates back to the 14th century, originally built as a hostel for pilgrims coming to Gloucester to visit the shrine of Edward II in the cathedral, and is reputed to be haunted by the spirit of a young girl. The sound of footsteps has been heard when no one else is there, and objects have been moved by an unseen hand, including a dog's bowl being turned over whilst the animal was eating, which frightened the dog so much that he ran to the other side of the room and refused to go back and finish his food.

Another of Gloucester's haunted pubs is the Coach and Horses in St Catherine Street, where the phantom of a little girl dressed in a white dress and pantaloons is said to linger. A former landlord of the pub told the Western Daily Press in 1997 that his family had been plagued by the sounds of banging and knocking, and had seen the ghostly girl.

The National Waterways Museum at Gloucester Docks is said to be haunted by a ghostly man dressed in black clothing. In 2008 a photograph taken by a teenage girl showed what seemed to be a blurred figure of a man, and visitors have reported hearing footsteps and mysterious voices around the museum when no one else is nearby…

GLOUCESTER, HARE LANE, FIRST SUNDAY SCHOOL 1892 29907

COACH & HORSES IN
THOMAS ENSTON
DEALER IN FOREIGN WINES
SPIRITS, BEER, CIDER & TOBA

Did You Know?
GLOUCESTER
A MISCELLANY

GLOUCESTER
THE CATHEDRAL
CLOISTER COURT
1891 28973

12

GLOUCESTER MISCELLANY

There used to be three legs of the River Severn running through Gloucester. The third channel silted up and vanished at some time in the 11th century.

Castle Mead derived its name from Gloucester Castle, mead being the Old English for the meadow, which is the other side of the River Severn from the castle. Nowadays it is referred to as Castle Meads.

St Mary de Lode church is the oldest church in Gloucester, dating from the 12th century.

In 1910 telephone numbers in Gloucester only had 3 digits. In 2004 we have 6 digits, plus a 5-digit dialling code.

In terms of overall area, the east window in Gloucester Cathedral is the largest window in any medieval cathedral in Britain. It measures 22 metres in height and is 12 metres wide, and the quire at the east end had to be widened for it to be of this great size. It was constructed in the 1350s and the colourful glass reflects medieval society of that time. For the monks of the cathedral it was their ornamental screen at the back of the altar.

Although it only took one tide for a ship to reach Gloucester it would take at least two tides to travel back down the Severn to the sea.

In June 2004 the 524th mayor of Gloucester was appointed. The position of sheriff goes back even farther than this!

GLOUCESTER, NEW INN COURTYARD 1893 32092A

GLOUCESTER, SOUTHGATE STREET, RAIKES HOUSE 1891 29006

GLOUCESTER, SOUTHGATE STREET 1891 29005

Queen Victoria was forced to change trains at Gloucester because there were two different-sized rail gauges on the route from the north to the south. So much luggage used to get mislaid that the city gained a reputation for 'Lost in Gloucester'.

At one time Gloucester had three psychiatric hospitals, ignorantly referred to as lunatic asylums.

Spa Road was named after saline water was discovered nearby. It could have been a spa town today if some clumsy workman hadn't fractured two adjacent pipes, one carrying the spa water, the other sewage!

Horse-drawn trams first appeared in the city in 1879, using attractive crimson and cream livery, operated by Gloucester City Tramways Company. Losing money, the company was taken over by the City of Gloucester Tramways Ltd in 1881. Their fortunes improved and the routes were extended. This continued until 1904, when electric trams were introduced into Gloucester, involving a major reconstruction of the system. The electric trams ran in Gloucester until they were discontinued in 1917.

GLOUCESTER, LONDON ROAD 1891 29007

In 1963 Gloucester Fire Brigade were called to a train crash at Tuffley. On arrival they found a large aircraft had crashed onto the roof of a house! The control room operator had mistaken 'plane' for 'train'.

Jews lived and worked in Eastgate Street before being sent to Bristol in the 1290s.

The United Reformed Church in Park Road was built in 1871 in memory of George Whitfield, who calculated that during his lifetime he had preached 1,800 sermons.

In the 1450s the population of Gloucester was only 4,000 compared to 110,500 in 2004.

The Germans sank the ninth HMS 'Gloucester' off Crete during World War II in 1941. The current (the tenth) HMS 'Gloucester' was launched at Southampton on 2 November 1982 by HRH the Duchess of Gloucester.

GLOUCESTER, FROM ROBINSWOOD HILL
1904 51985

GLOUCESTER, NORTHGATE STREET 1904 51988

Did You Know?
GLOUCESTER
A MISCELLANY

GLOUCESTER, EASTGATE STREET 1931 83828

An oak tree was planted in Gloucester Park on 4th August 1902 in celebration of the coronation of King Edward VII.

A lifeboat was launched in Gloucester Docks on 9 April 1867. It was named 'Gloucester' and, following the launch, taken to Falmouth for service with the RNLI.

GLOUCESTER, BISHOP HOOPER'S LODGING AND MUSEUM 1949 G20016

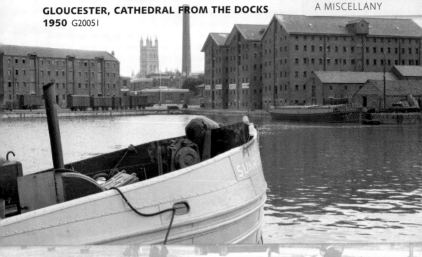

GLOUCESTER, CATHEDRAL FROM THE DOCKS
1950 G20051

During the 1850s the length of railway track in Britain doubled and by 1875 doubled again. Rolling stock was required, and in 1860 the Gloucester Wagon Co Ltd began in buildings in an area now known as the Peel Centre, off the Bristol Road, alongside the Gloucester & Sharpness Canal. They employed 120 men, manufacturing for their first order 1,000 coal wagons for the West Midland Railway Co. By 1867 their first foreign order was completed, 500 wagons for the Great Indian Peninsular Railway. Orders for Russia and Buenos Aires soon followed. In 1887, 20 years after this, the company was renamed the Gloucester Railway Carriage and Wagon Co Ltd, although it was popularly known as 'the Wagon Works'. The most luxurious coach ever built was for His Excellency the Maharajah Holkar of Indore in 1936. Sadly the Maharajah Holkar never saw it, as he was overthrown from power before delivery! During the First World War the Wagon Works was used as a munitions factory and in 1915 a parade was held through the city to recruit workers. Orders began to decline in the mid 20th century, and in 1989 the works buildings were demolished to make way for Toys R Us.

MAISEMORE, THE BRIDGE 1906 55840

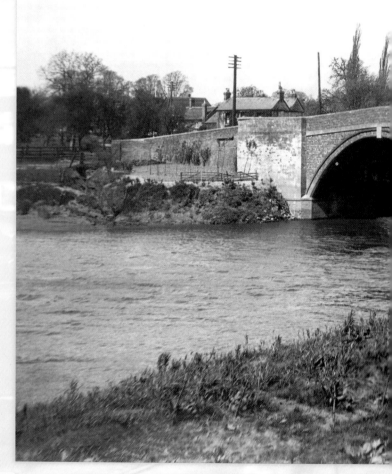

The River Severn produces the highest bore in Europe.

GLOUCESTER, SOUTHGATE STREET 1904 51987

'The Citizen', Gloucester's newspaper, first appeared on 1 May 1876. It was four pages long and cost one halfpenny.

The Gloucester Chamber of Commerce was founded in 1839 to become the principal businessman's association in the city.

The Theatre de Luxe cinema in Northgate Street was once a piano factory for Frederick Goddard.

Bearland was originally an open site in front of the castle and in the Middle Ages used as a dumping ground for refuse.

The Oxebode used to be called Mitre Street in the 19th century. During this period it became a slum.

St Aldate Street was named after a medieval church that used to stand on the south side of the street until it was demolished in the mid 17th century.

GLOUCESTER, SOUTHGATE STREET 1949 G20014

Bull Lane is another street that has changed its name during the course of time. In the 13th century it was called Gore Lane.

The Bon Marche shop was opened in 1889 as a drapery business, and was to become Gloucester's largest departmental store. In the early 1970s it became a Debenham's store.

The Mariners' Church was built in the docks in 1849 as a mission to the numerous seamen who visited the port.

Salt was the only regular export out of Gloucester Docks. It came down the Severn in small boats to be loaded onto ships in the docks.

Henry III was crowned in 1216 in the Abbey of St Peter, Gloucester, rather than in Westminster Abbey, because of civil unrest in England.

King Henry VIII with his wife Anne Boleyn visited Gloucester in 1535 as the guest of the Abbot of St Peter.

St Mary's Gate was built in the 12th century and was the main entrance to the abbey of St Peter. It is said that people gathered at the windows in 1555 to watch Bishop Hooper burn at the stake (see page 32).

**GLOUCESTER, WESTGATE STREET AND ST NICHOLAS' CHURCH
1949** G20024

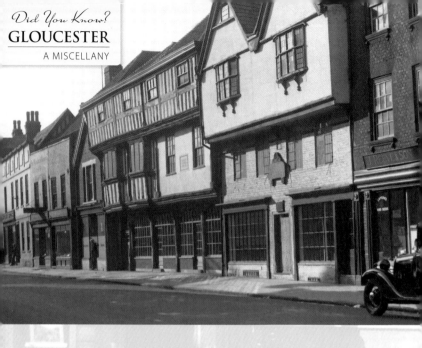

GLOUCESTER, BISHOP HOOPER'S LODGING AND MUSEUM 1936
87385

In the 16th century Gloucester, like many other places in Britain, was caught up in the troubles over religious issues between Catholic and Protestant forms of Christianity. When the Catholic Queen Mary came to the throne she ruthlessly tried to suppress Protestantism in England, and three Protestant martyrs met gruesome deaths in Gloucester by being burnt at the stake, one of whom was John Hooper, Bishop of Gloucester. Photograph 87385 (above) shows the building in Lower Westgate Street in Gloucester where Bishop Hooper is believed to have lodged before his martyrdom; it is now home to Gloucester Folk Museum. In 1862 a monument was built on the spot in St Mary's Square on which Bishop Hooper died in 1555. A memorial now marks the reputed spot of Bishop Hooper's execution.

The longest railway platform in England is at Gloucester Railway Station. It is 602.6 metres long (six times longer than a football pitch).

In c1960 Walls Ice-cream built the largest ice-cream factory in Europe at Barnwood.

GLOUCESTER, ART GALLERY 1912 65116

Sir Charles Wheatstone was born in Westgate Street. He invented the electric telegraph and later was involved in laying the first transatlantic telegraph cable.

Gloucester has been the location of many epic films and TV series. Recently scenes from the famous Harry Potter films were shot in Gloucester Cathedral. Others have included 'The Onedin Line', 'Buffalo Girls' and 'The Choir'.

Gloucester Cathedral has been rated as the seventh most beautiful cathedral in the world. The cathedral has a Norman nave, later Gothic vaulting, an early Perpendicular choir and a later Perpendicular Lady Chapel; yet these disparate architectural styles form a coherent whole. William Froucester, a renowned figure in the history of the building, completed the cloisters after 1381. It is one of the most perfect structures of its kind in existence, shown in photograph 28997 below.

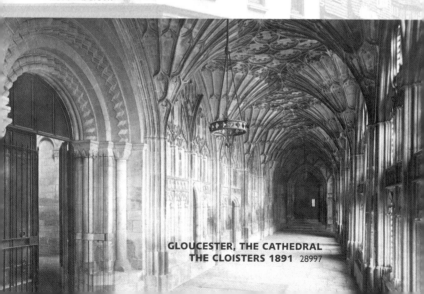

**GLOUCESTER, THE CATHEDRAL
THE CLOISTERS 1891** 28997

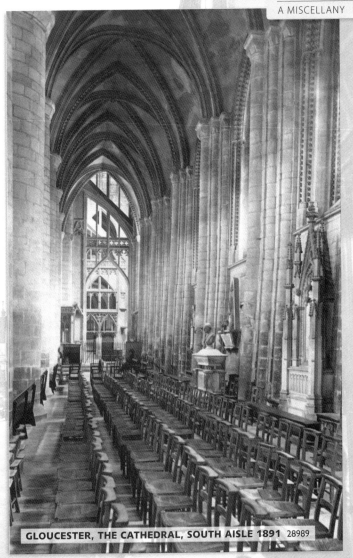

GLOUCESTER, THE CATHEDRAL, SOUTH AISLE 1891 28989

GLOUCESTER, WESTGATE STREET 1912 65109

Beatrix Potter chose a tiny shop in College Court (just off Westgate Street) as the setting for her story 'The Tailor of Gloucester'. The shop is now The Tailor of Gloucester Beatrix Potter Museum and Shop.

George Whitfield preached his first sermon from the pulpit of St Mart de Crypt Church in 1736.

The inventor of the vacuum cleaner was Hubert Cecil Booth, born in Gloucester in 1871.

GLOUCESTER, WESTGATE BRIDGE 1906 55843

Bones were discovered at Barnwood gravel pits (where the Walls Ice-cream factory is) belonging to mammoths and woolly rhinoceroses, plus tools made by humans perhaps 250,000 years ago.

King Henry II granted Gloucester its first royal charter in 1155, acknowledging the city's equal status with London and Winchester.

GLOUCESTER, EASTGATE STREET 1950 G20047

GLOUCESTER, THE CATHEDRAL
NORTH EAST 1891 28970

An important local industry in Gloucester in the past was pin making. This began in the 17th century in various premises dotted around the city. Men, women and children worked in cramped and dirty conditions for six days a week making small pins by hand. One of the largest employers was John Tilsley, who in 1632 employed 80 boys and girls. One building used was the upper floor of what is now Gloucester's Folk Museum in Westgate Street, where today they still find pins under the floorboards.

The oldest inn in Gloucester, known in 1455 as the 'New Inn', is still called by the same name. It was built specially to cater for pilgrims visiting the Abbey of St Peter.

GLOUCESTER, ROBERT RAIKES SUNDAY SCHOOL 1949 G20015

GLOUCESTER, WESTGATE STREET 1948 G20003

GLOUCESTER, LOWER NORTHGATE 1923 73668

SPORTING GLOUCESTER

A Gloucester man surfing the Severn Bore, Dave Lawson, achieved the world surfing record when he rode the Bore for 5.7 miles on 29th August 1996.

Gloucestershire County Cricket Club reached the record for the highest score in county cricket at Gloucester on 12 June 2004. New Zealand batsman Craig Spearman reached a score of 341 against Middlesex, hitting 40 fours and 6 sixes. Gloucestershire's own W G Grace, who scored 318 in 1876, held the previous record.

Gloucester boasts one of the oldest and most famous of all rugby clubs in England. The club was formed from a meeting at the Spread Eagle Hotel in 1873, and the team played at the Spa on the current cricket ground. A tradition of the club was that only local players were eligible to play, something that lasted to the end of the 20th century when the famous 'Cherry and Whites' of Gloucester RFC turned professional. In 1891 the club purchased land at Kingsholm for £4,000 from Castle Grim estates. Since then the club has gone from strength to strength, with players regularly being selected to play for England. There were three Gloucester Rugby Club players in the England Rugby World Cup-winning squad in 2003: Phil Vickery, Trevor Woodman and Andy Gomarsall.

Gloucester is the home of one of the more unusual sports played in Britain – American Football. The Gloucester Banshees American Football Club, based at the Oxstalls Tennis Centre, plays at national level in the British American Football League.

Gloucester City Football Club, nicknamed 'The Tigers', can trace its origins back to 1883. The club was originally formed as 'Gloucester FC', but had become 'Gloucester City FC' by the mid 1920s. The club's first recorded match, in January 1886, was refereed by none other than Gloucestershire's legendary cricketing hero W G Grace. Until the end of the 2008/09 season, when Gloucester City won promotion to the Conference North, the club were the longest serving members of the Southern Football League, having played in the league for 68 consecutive seasons.

QUIZ QUESTIONS

Answers on page 50.

1. What was the Roman name for Gloucester?

2. Can you name the two channels of the River Severn that pass through Gloucester today?

3. Photograph 28972 (opposite) shows the south porch of Gloucester Cathedral. Carved figures of the 7th-century Anglo-Saxon King Osric and Serlo, the 11th-century Abbot of Gloucester, are on either side of the entrance, but who do the six figures over the doorway represent?

4. What can be found in Gloucester Cathedral in memory of Robert, Duke of Normandy, William the Conqueror's eldest son?

5. Which former Mayor of London has a pub in Gloucester named after him?

6. What is the name of someone who comes from Gloucester?

7. Which famous motor cycles were once manufactured in Gloucester?

8. What famous cultural event takes place every three years in Gloucester?

9. Which four towns around the world are twinned with Gloucester, and where are they?

10. What was the Gloster Gladiator?

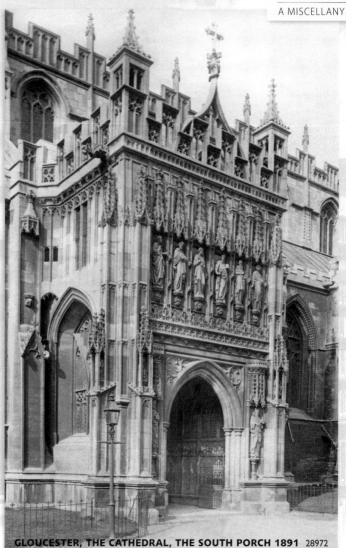

GLOUCESTER, THE CATHEDRAL, THE SOUTH PORCH 1891 28972

RECIPE

CHESTNUT SOUP

Chestnuts are said to have been introduced to Britain by the Romans. The Gloucestershire area is rich in Roman remains, and there is a saying 'scratch Gloucestershire and find Rome'. The city of Gloucester itself stands on the site of an old Roman fort and was an important town in Roman times. This makes an ideal soup for Christmas time. A tin of chestnut purée can also be used if preferred, instead of chestnuts.

> 450g/1 lb chestnuts
> 1.2 litres/2 pints chicken or vegetable stock
> 4 tablespoonfuls cream
> 25g/1oz butter
> ¼ teaspoonful white pepper
> ½ teaspoonful salt
> ½ teaspoonful caster sugar
> A blade of mace, or a pinch of ground mace

Cut the ends off the chestnuts, and roast them in a moderate oven (180°C/350°F/Gas Mark 4) for about 20 minutes, until the outer and inner skins will peel off easily. Remove all the skins and then put the chestnuts in a saucepan with the vegetable stock, white pepper, salt, pepper, mace and caster sugar. Simmer all together for 1 hour or longer, until the chestnuts are quite tender.

When the chestnuts are cooked, take out the blade of mace and discard. Rub the chestnuts through a fine sieve (or put through a blender), moistening them with a little of the stock. Rinse out the saucepan, and return the chestnut purée and stock to it. Add the cream, and bring the soup to just below boiling point, stirring well, then reduce heat, cover the pan and simmer gently for about 20 minutes, until it is quite smooth – it should have the consistency of thin cream, but add a little milk or stock if it is too thick. Check for seasoning, and adjust to taste if necessary.

RECIPE

GLOUCESTER TARTS

175g/6oz shortcrust pastry
50g/2oz butter or margarine
50g/2oz caster sugar
1 egg
1 teaspoonful almond essence
50g/2oz ground rice
Raspberry jam

Pre-heat the oven to 180°C/350°F/Gas Mark 4.

Grease some patty tins. Roll out the pastry on a lightly-floured surface and cut it into rounds about 5cm (2 inch) in diameter, and use the rounds to line the patty tins.

Cream the sugar and butter or margarine together until light and fluffy. Beat the egg and carefully add it to the creamed mixture, a little at a time. Stir in the almond essence and the ground rice and mix all the ingredients thoroughly together.

Put a spoonful of jam into the bottom of each patty tin, and then cover with a good spoonful of the mixture. Bake the tarts in the pre-heated oven for about 20 minutes, until the filling is firm and lightly golden. Leave to cool before eating.

QUIZ ANSWERS

1. Glevum. In AD97 'Glevum'was designated as a 'Colonia' – the highest urban status in the Roman Empire.

2. The East Channel and West Channel of the Parting.

3. The figures over the doorway of the south porch of the cathedral represent Saint Peter, Saint Paul, and the four evangelists, the Saints Matthew, Mark, Luke and John.

4. A coloured wooden effigy of him in full armour. Robert of Normandy, also known as Robert Curthose, died at Cardiff Castle in 1134 and was buried in the abbey church of St Peter in Gloucester, which later became Gloucester Cathedral. The exact place of his burial is not known, but his effigy on a mortuary chest can be found in the cathedral.

5. Dick Whittington, who was born in Gloucestershire, at Pauntley in the Forest of Dean and became Mayor of London three times, in 1397, 1406 and in 1419. He has since been portrayed in many Christmas pantomimes. In the 15th century Richard Whittington, Lord of Staunton, occupied St Nicholas House in Westgate Street in Gloucester and was probably Dick Whittington's nephew. St Nicholas House is now one of the city's popular public houses, and is aptly named the Dick Whittington.

6. A Gloucestrian.

7. Cotton Motorcycles. The Cotton Motorcycle Company was founded by Frank Willoughby Cotton in Gloucester in1918. The company was later reconstituted as E Cotton (Motorcycles) Ltd, and traded till 1980, when the factory was closed. The Cotton Owners and Enthusiasts Club now holds an annual rally of Cotton motorcycles at the Gloucester Folk Museum every summer.

8. The Three Choirs Festival. In the early 1700s the choirs of the three cathedral cities of Hereford, Worcester and Goucester decided to hold a 'musick meeting'. The event is still held annually, now known as the Three Choirs Festival, and is hosted by the three cities in turn. It is said to be the oldest non-competitive music festival in Europe, as opposed to festivals for other purposes where music is played. The name 'festival' was applied from 1837, and it evolved from something purely choral to the inclusion of instrumental works.

9. Metz in France, Trier in Germany, Gouda in The Netherlands, and St Ann in Jamaica.

10. The Gloster Gladiator was a famous biplane fighter aircraft that was manufactured by the Gloster Aircraft Company, known locally as GAC. During the First World War a large expanse of land encroaching both Hucclecote and Brockworth had been used as the Air Band acceptance park. After the war small aircraft were being built in Cheltenham, but because of increasing orders the manufacturers were forced to look for a larger site. In 1928 the Gloucestershire Aircraft Company moved to the airfield at Hucclecote and became one of Britain's well-respected industries. In 1926, the name of the company was changed to the Gloster Aircraft Company. Between 1941 and 1945 a staggering 3,330 aeroplanes were built at Hucclecote. Indeed, this was part of the development of the first jet aircraft and the question is still asked, 'Did the first jet aeroplane fly from here?' Actually the first Gloster E.28/39 (Whittle Jet) made short hops down the runway on 8 May 1941 before being taken by road to RAF Cranwell, where the first flight was made on 15 May. As well as the Gloster Gladiator, other notable aircraft produced at the factory included the Hawker Typhoon, Gloster Meteor, and the Javelin. Moreton Valence Airfield, located about five miles west of Gloucester, was used for the assembly of Javelins and a base for the test flight of the aircraft. In 1956 the Javelin programme was cancelled, and to keep trading GAC began designing and building vending machines, forage harvesters, fire engines and road tankers. Finally on 6 April 1964 the Hucclecote factory was sold and the site became Gloucester Trading Estate. Today nothing remains of the old buildings and hangars of this once important local industry.

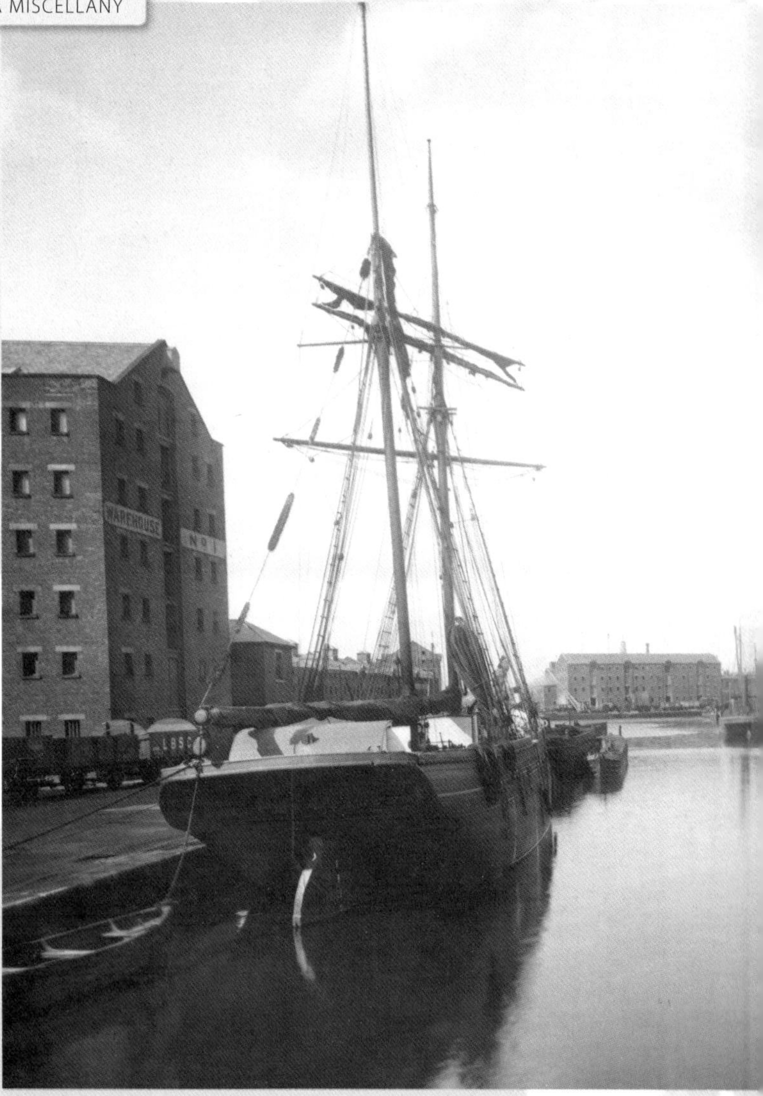
WAREHOUSE
No 1
LBSC

GLOUCESTER, THE DOCKS 1923 73689

FRANCIS FRITH

PIONEER VICTORIAN PHOTOGRAPHER

Francis Frith, founder of the world-famous photographic archive, was a complex and multi-talented man. A devout Quaker and a highly successful Victorian businessman, he was philosophical by nature and pioneering in outlook. By 1855 he had already established a wholesale grocery business in Liverpool, and sold it for the astonishing sum of £200,000, which is the equivalent today of over £15,000,000. Now in his thirties, and captivated by the new science of photography, Frith set out on a series of pioneering journeys up the Nile and to the Near East.

INTRIGUE AND EXPLORATION

He was the first photographer to venture beyond the sixth cataract of the Nile. Africa was still the mysterious 'Dark Continent', and Stanley and Livingstone's historic meeting was a decade into the future. The conditions for picture taking confound belief. He laboured for hours in his wicker dark-room in the sweltering heat of the desert, while the volatile chemicals fizzed dangerously in their trays. Back in London he exhibited his photographs and was 'rapturously cheered' by members of the Royal Society. His reputation as a photographer was made overnight.

VENTURE OF A LIFE-TIME

By the 1870s the railways had threaded their way across the country, and Bank Holidays and half-day Saturdays had been made obligatory by Act of Parliament. All of a sudden the working man and his family were able to enjoy days out, take holidays, and see a little more of the world.

With typical business acumen, Francis Frith foresaw that these new tourists would enjoy having souvenirs to commemorate their days out. For the next thirty years he travelled the country by train and by pony and trap, producing fine photographs of seaside resorts and beauty spots that were keenly bought by millions of Victorians. These prints were painstakingly pasted into family albums and pored over during the dark nights of winter, rekindling precious memories of summer excursions. Frith's studio was soon supplying retail shops all over the country, and by 1890 F Frith & Co had become the greatest specialist photographic publishing company in the world, with over 2,000 sales outlets, and pioneered the picture postcard.

FRANCIS FRITH'S LEGACY

Francis Frith had died in 1898 at his villa in Cannes, his great project still growing. By 1970 the archive he created contained over a third of a million pictures showing 7,000 British towns and villages.

Frith's legacy to us today is of immense significance and value, for the magnificent archive of evocative photographs he created provides a unique record of change in the cities, towns and villages throughout Britain over a century and more. Frith and his fellow studio photographers revisited locations many times down the years to update their views, compiling for us an enthralling and colourful pageant of British life and character.

We are fortunate that Frith was dedicated to recording the minutiae of everyday life. For it is this sheer wealth of visual data, the painstaking chronicle of changes in dress, transport, street layouts, buildings, housing and landscape that captivates us so much today, offering us a powerful link with the past and with the lives of our ancestors.

Computers have now made it possible for Frith's many thousands of images to be accessed almost instantly. The archive offers every one of us an opportunity to examine the places where we and our families have lived and worked down the years. Its images, depicting our shared past, are now bringing pleasure and enlightenment to millions around the world a century and more after his death.

For further information visit: www.francisfrith.com

INTERIOR DECORATION

Frith's photographs can be seen framed and as giant wall murals in thousands of pubs, restaurants, hotels, banks, retail stores and other public buildings throughout Britain. These provide interesting and attractive décor, generating strong local interest and acting as a powerful reminder of gentler days in our increasingly busy and frenetic world.

FRITH PRODUCTS

All Frith photographs are available as prints and posters in a variety of different sizes and styles. In the UK we also offer a range of other gift and stationery products illustrated with Frith photographs, although many of these are not available for delivery outside the UK – see our web site for more information on the products available for delivery in your country.

THE INTERNET

Over 100,000 photographs of Britain can be viewed and purchased on the Frith web site. The web site also includes memories and reminiscences contributed by our customers, who have personal knowledge of localities and of the people and properties depicted in Frith photographs. If you wish to learn more about a specific town or village you may find these reminiscences fascinating to browse. Why not add your own comments if you think they would be of interest to others? See **www.francisfrith.com**

PLEASE HELP US BRING FRITH'S PHOTOGRAPHS TO LIFE

Our authors do their best to recount the history of the places they write about. They give insights into how particular towns and villages developed, they describe the architecture of streets and buildings, and they discuss the lives of famous people who lived there. But however knowledgeable our authors are, the story they tell is necessarily incomplete.

Frith's photographs are so much more than plain historical documents. They are living proofs of the flow of human life down the generations. They show real people at real moments in history; and each of those people is the son or daughter of someone, the brother or sister, aunt or uncle, grandfather or grandmother of someone else. All of them lived, worked and played in the streets depicted in Frith's photographs.

We would be grateful if you would give us your insights into the places shown in our photographs: the streets and buildings, the shops, businesses and industries. Post your memories of life in those streets on the Frith website: what it was like growing up there, who ran the local shop and what shopping was like years ago; if your workplace is shown tell us about your working day and what the building is used for now. Read other visitors' memories and reconnect with your shared local history and heritage. With your help more and more Frith photographs can be brought to life, and vital memories preserved for posterity, and for the benefit of historians in the future.

Wherever possible, we will try to include some of your comments in future editions of our books. Moreover, if you spot errors in dates, titles or other facts, please let us know, because our archive records are not always completely accurate—they rely on 140 years of human endeavour and hand-compiled records. You can email us using the contact form on the website.

Thank you!

For further information, trade, or author enquiries
please contact us at the address below:

**The Francis Frith Collection, 6 Oakley Business Park,
Wylye Road, Dinton, Salisbury, Wiltshire, England SP3 5EU.**
Tel: +44 (0)1722 716 376 Fax: +44 (0)1722 716 881
e-mail: sales@francisfrith.co.uk **www.francisfrith.com**